EXCELLENCE
PLAYBOOK

FELLOWSHIP OF CHRISTIAN ATHLETES

EXCELLENCE
PLAYBOOK

TRUE CHAMPIONS TALK ABOUT
THE HEART AND SOUL IN SPORTS

Revell

a division of Baker Publishing Group
Grand Rapids, Michigan

© 2016 by Fellowship of Christian Athletes

Published by Revell
a division of Baker Publishing Group
P.O. Box 6287, Grand Rapids, MI 49516–6287
www.revellbooks.com

Material adapted from *Excellence*, published in 2009 by Regal Books

ISBN 978-0-8007-2693-5

Printed in the United States of America

16 17 18 19 20 21 22   7 6 5 4 3 2 1

Contents

The Four Core

DAN BRITTON

Executive Vice President of International Ministry, Fellowship of Christian Athletes

The NCAA Final Four tournament is an exciting sporting event. Even if you are not a person who likes basketball, it is awesome to watch March Madness as it narrows down sixty-four teams into four core teams. This makes me think about Fellowship of Christian Athlete's "Four Core"—not four core teams, but four core values.

Core values are simply the way you live and conduct yourself. They are your attitudes, beliefs, and convictions. Values should be what you are, not what you want to become. The goal is to embody your values every step of the way.

Are your values just words, or do you actually live them out? Can others identify the values in your life without your telling them? Your values need to be a driving force that shapes the way you do life! Talk is cheap, but values are valuable.

When everything is stripped away, what is left? For FCA, it is integrity, serving, teamwork, and excellence. These Four Core are so powerful to me that I have made them my own personal values. So, I have to ask you, what are your values? What guides you? Let me share with you FCA's Four Core, which are even better than the Final Four!

Integrity

To have integrity means that you are committed to Christlike wholeness, both privately and publicly. Basically, it means to live without gaps. Proverbs 11:3 says that integrity should guide you, but that a double life will destroy you. You need to be transparent, authentic, honest, and trustworthy. You should be the same in all situations and not become someone different when the competition of the game begins. Integrity means to act the same when no one is looking as you do when all eyes are on you. It is not about being perfect, but, as a coach or athlete, you need to be the real deal.

Serving

In John 13:12–15, Jesus gives us the perfect example of serving when He washes the disciples' feet. He then commands the disciples to go and do unto others what

He has done to them. How many of your
teammates' feet have you washed? Maybe
not literally, but spiritually, do you have
an attitude of serving just as if you were
washing their feet in the locker room? You
need to seek out the needs of others and
be passionate about pursuing people who
are needy. And, the last time I checked,
everyone is needy.

Teamwork

Teamwork means to work together
with others and express unity in Christ
in all of your relationships. In Philip-
pians 2:1–5, Paul encourages each of
us to be one, united together in spirit
and purpose. We all need to be on one
team—not just the team we play on,
but on God's Team! We need to equip,
encourage, and empower one another.
Do you celebrate and hurt together as
teammates? You need to be arm-in-arm
with others, locking up together to

accomplish God's work. There should be no Lone Rangers.

Excellence

To pursue excellence means to honor and glorify God in everything you do. In Colossians 3:23–24, Paul writes, "whatever you do, work at it with all your heart, as working for the Lord, not for human masters" (NIV). The "whatever" part is hard, because it means that everything you do must be done for God, not others. You need to pursue excellence in practice, in games, in schoolwork, and in lifting weights. God deserves your best, not your leftovers.

It is tip-off time for the game of life. How will you be known?

> Whatever happens, conduct yourselves in a manner worthy of the gospel of Christ.
>
> Philippians 1:27 NIV

Introduction

Leave a Mark

I have been crucified with Christ and I no longer live, but Christ lives in me. The life I live in the body, I live by faith in the Son of God, who loved me and gave himself for me.

Galatians 2:20 NIV

Lord Jesus, my prayer is to live and compete with integrity, serving, teamwork, and excellence. It is a high standard, but I know that with Your power and strength, it can happen. I want all my relationships to be known for things that are of You. Search my heart and reveal to me my values. I lay at the foot of the cross the values that do not honor You, and I ask for Your forgiveness. The values that bring You glory, I lay them at the foot of the cross for Your anointing.

An imprint is a permanent mark. To make an imprint means to engrave, etch, impress, or inscribe. When I was eight years old, I had a once-in-a-lifetime opportunity to ride my older brother's motorcycle. Wanting to show him how big and tough I was, I took off at full speed. Less than one hundred yards down the dirt road, the cycle's front tire hit a hole, which sent me flying. I landed in a nearby ditch, and the motorcycle landed on my back. Talk about painful!

Fortunately, the curve of the ditch allowed most of my body to be spared from the impact. The only part of the motorcycle that was touching me was the muffler, which was pressing into my back. Unfortunately, since it was hot, the muffler burned through my shirt and my flesh, and I experienced a new level of pain. My brother came quickly to my rescue, which spared me from being seriously wounded. I was, however, banned from riding his bike ever again. And even though the wreck happened more than thirty years ago, I still have a nice burn mark on my back—the imprint of that hot muffler.

Think about this: Every time we compete, coach, or lead, we leave an imprint. Whether it is a positive or a negative impression is up to us. When we are committed to excellence, we naturally desire to leave the kind of mark on others that will have an eternal impact. As a part of this commitment, we all, as followers of Christ, need to be intentional in striving, straining, and stretching to give our very best in all areas.

When I was younger, I was shown what it meant to leave an imprint of excellence. My grandfather, "Pop," showed me what it meant to pursue excellence by staying spiritually hungry. One month before he died, I went to visit Pop at his home. As we talked in his living room, I noticed three items he kept on his end table: a large-print Bible, a magnifying glass, and a tape recorder.

I knew that his eyesight had been failing for years, which accounted for the first two things, but the tape recorder puzzled me. Out of curiosity, I asked him about it. His answer astonished me. "This is where I meet God every morning," he said, "and unfortunately by the end of the day, I sometimes forget what He taught me from His Word. I decided that if I read the Bible *and* listened to it on tape, I'd double my chance of remembering it." My grandfather was spiritually hungry and was willing to do whatever it took to feed that desire. He was pursuing excellence to the very end.

When it comes to the pursuit of excellence, the ultimate question is not whether we leave a good or bad imprint, but whether we leave an imprint of ourselves or of Jesus. What a challenge! My grandfather certainly left an imprint of Christ on me, and I must continually ask myself if I am doing the same for others.

Whether we are playing or coaching or leading, we all must be committed to excellence and to leaving behind the imprint of Christ. What about you? Do you pursue excellence? Are you marking others with excellence? Give the Lord what's right, not what's left. Leave a mark—or, better yet, leave an imprint of Jesus. That is a true reflection of a commitment to excellence.

How to Use This Book

Excellence Playbook takes an in-depth look at this core value and comes at it from six different angles as lived out by six different people. Their insights shed new light on this value and give us a model to follow.

You can read *Excellence Playbook* individually or as part of a group. As part of a personal devotion time, you can gain insight as you read through each story and ponder the "Training Time" questions at the end. Mentors can also use this book in a discipleship relationship, using the "Training Time" questions to step up conversations to the next level. And small groups (Huddles) can study the core value as a group to be prepared to sharpen each other with questions.

1

The Big Win

TONY DUNGY

*Winning Super Bowl Coach
of the Indianapolis Colts*

Don't you know that the runners in a stadium all race, but only one receives the prize? Run in such a way to win the prize.

1 Corinthians 9:24

For when the One Great Scorer comes to write against your name, He marks—not that you won or lost—but how you played the Game.

Grantland Rice,
"Alumnus Football"

From the peewee leagues to the professional ranks, there is one constant truth when it comes to coaching: practice makes perfect.

No better example of this time-tested principle can be found than with former Indianapolis Colts' head coach Tony

Dungy. Known for practicing what he preaches (although saying the soft-spoken leader preaches would be somewhat of a stretch), Dungy, who now serves as an analyst on NBC's *Sunday Night Football*, has taken his disciplined methods beyond the football field and into his personal life. That's why he is such a strong proponent of the Fellowship of Christian Athletes' four core values.

"If you just practice one day a week, you're never going to be as good as if you practice every day," Dungy says. "And that's what it's all about, really. It's reading and understanding what God wants you to do and then putting it into practice. When you come up a little short and don't quite get it, don't give up. Continue to work at it. Say, 'Okay, Lord, I fell a little bit short in this area. Give me another opportunity so that I can continue to work on it.' The more you practice those values, the easier they become, and the better you get at them."

Of those four core values, Dungy has especially been equated with excellence throughout his coaching career. It's a characteristic that has shone brightly during his greatest victory (Super Bowl XLI in 2007) and his greatest tragedy (the passing of his oldest son, James, in 2005).

Former Colts linebacker Tyjuan Hagler—who played for Dungy from 2005 to 2009—is one of the many eyewitnesses to that fact. "I've learned a lot about how strong his faith is," Hagler says. "When the tragedy occurred, we went down [to Tampa] for the funeral. When we were waiting, we were seated in this room; and when he walked through the door, he had the biggest smile on his face. I was just thinking, *He's got the biggest smile on his face, and he is just hurting so bad inside.* That really touched me."

Hagler likewise experienced Super Bowl bliss with the Colts in February 2007 and can honestly attest to Dungy's even-keeled approach to excellence. "He's the same guy," he says. "When we won the championship, he praised God. He gave the honor to Christ, and he said that without Christ, none of us would be here right now. He did the same thing when he lost his son that he did when we won the Super Bowl. He put both situations in God's hands."

FCA president and CEO Les Steckel has likewise observed Dungy over the years and gotten a firsthand look at Dungy's quest for excellence. Steckel was the offensive coordinator for the Tampa Bay Buccaneers in 2000 when Dungy served as that team's head (1996 to 2000).

"One thing that people don't understand about coaching in the NFL is the tremendous pressures," Steckel says. "Tony Dungy taught me a great deal about handling those. Under all the pressure, I knew that his stomach was turning, but his demeanor was awesome. That countenance that he continues to display to this day was one that we all wish we had in pressure-packed times in our lives."

According to former NFL head coach and current ESPN analyst Herman Edwards—who was an assistant coach at Tampa Bay from 1996 to 2000—Dungy also displayed excellence by readily taking responsibility for the team's failures.

"Anytime we had a bad day on defense, people would ask him what happened, and he'd just say, 'Well, we just have to tackle a little bit better,'" Edwards recalls. "He never ran down the players out there. He would just say that we needed to coach them a little better, and at the end of the day, he was right. That's what we needed to do better."

Tampa Bay cornerback Ronde Barber, who played for Dungy from 1996 to 2000, uncovered another aspect of the excellence Dungy strives for: patience. Dungy is a great exhibitor of this characteristic, which is spoken of in Proverbs 19:11—"A person's wisdom yields patience; it is to one's glory to overlook an offense" (NIV).

"Not everything is solved with haste and urgency," Barber agrees. "You can be urgent and patient at the same time. Tony was always good at keeping everything in perspective."

Perhaps the most astute observation of Dungy comes from running back Shaun Alexander, who clearly recognizes the role that one's purpose in life plays in relation to excellence.

"[Dungy] accepts the calling he has been given," Alexander says. "He is called to glorify God and be a champion. He walks it, talks it, lives it. You see it in his eyes. He will compete and fight until the end, all the while smiling at his opponents."

Dungy's definition of excellence, on the other hand, is a bit more straightforward and, true to coaching form, textbook in nature.

"Excellence is doing something at the very highest level it can be done using all your capabilities and everything God has given you," Dungy says. "Sometimes that gets lost. We don't always think of excellence as a Christian concept, but I think God does desire us to be excellent at what we do."

Dungy can think of many examples of excellence in athletics, such as legendary head coach Chuck Noll, for whom he played at Pittsburgh from 1977 to 1978. But in his mind, no one can surpass the level of excellence that his parents, Wilbur and CleoMae Dungy, modeled for him growing up in Jackson, Michigan. "My parents were definitions of excellence in teaching," Dungy says. "It was important to them to be the best that they could be—not for personal reasons but because that was their concept of serving. They wanted to serve people in the best way possible."

"I think excellence is something we have to be cognizant of," he adds. "Just because we're Christians doesn't mean we should take the approach to just move forward and let the Lord handle it. We do have a responsibility to be the very best we can be in whatever field we decide to take up."

Dungy believes that Christ-centered excellence is usually either taught incorrectly (with the emphasis being toward personal benefit as opposed to God's glory) or isn't taught at all. His first exposure to the concept came at an FCA camp where he learned about Paul's athletic reference in 1 Corinthians 9:24–27. In particular, Dungy was drawn to verse 24, which says, "Run in such a way to win the prize."

"That's the first time it hit me that, according to the Bible, we aren't supposed to be satisfied with mediocrity or think that winning is the wrong goal to have," Dungy recalls. "It says run to win, but understand what the prize is and understand that we've got to compete for spiritual things and long-lasting things. There's nothing wrong with being excellent, and that verse has always stuck out to me."

One of the dangers of achieving excellence comes in the form of pride—that is, when the individual who has achieved success because of their excellence takes the credit and in turn uses it for their own personal gain. Dungy has seen this play out in the lives of many athletes and has likewise seen the shallow results.

"If you're running to win, but you have only earthly goals in mind, it will be short-lived," Dungy says. "It will be a withering type of thing. You have to have those spiritual goals in mind. Things do get in the way of being excellent. Some of those things are pride and self-centeredness, but you still have to do everything as unto the Lord. You have to try to keep those types of thoughts out."

Dungy also says our purpose behind striving for excellence must always be balanced and in tune with God's plan for our lives. Otherwise, we might become like the rich man Jesus talks about in the parable He shares in Luke 12:13–21.

The landowner, blessed with a bountiful crop, decides to build bigger barns for his abundance and then says that he will "take it easy" (v. 19). But the rich man is in for a rude awakening: "God said to him, 'You fool! This very night your life is demanded of you. And the things you have prepared—whose will they be?'" (v. 20).

"That's where you have to understand what's spiritual and what's long-lasting," Dungy says. "Where is your soul? That's the thing that's going to last. We do have misguided priorities if we're just thinking only in terms of excellence. Everything has to balance out. Excellence without service or excellence without teamwork is excellence for only your purpose. It all has to come into balance."

For coaches and athletes, excellence is often defined in terms of wins and losses. Those who find themselves in the winner's circle are deemed excellent by virtue of their accomplishment, while those who struggle to win often have their excellence questioned.

Similar yardsticks are used in other areas of life. Business, entertainment, arts, science, fashion, and most everything in popular culture are all judged by the world's standard of success, which creates a tricky road that must be carefully maneuvered—especially for believers and followers of Christ.

"You have to try to keep your priorities straight," Dungy says. "You have to look at the world from a Christian point of view, which isn't always easy to do. There are going to be times when you don't win. There are going to be times when you get fired, and you can't let that affect your self-esteem. You can't let it affect your outlook, because we have to measure ourselves by a different standard than the world's standard."

Dungy believes that wins and losses are one of sports' great inspirations to excellence, but he also fully understands the danger that lies within that dynamic. For instance, too often society falls into the trap of demeaning and devaluing anyone who fails to reach a certain level of success. With that in mind, Dungy focuses on performance and effort more than the final result.

"We do have a scoreboard that measures the final tally of the game," he says. "But we don't all have the same opportunities. We don't all have the same talent. So to me, more than the scoreboard, I like to focus on how our team is doing. Are we doing everything we can? Are we using all of the ability that God has given us?

"There will be days for my football team when we win that I'm not happy because we didn't really play excellently, we didn't practice as well as we can, we didn't use those talents. There are other games when we lose and I have to say, 'You know what? We gave it everything we had. We did as much as we could do. It just wasn't our day today, but I'm really proud of our team.' To me, it's more about knowing what my potential is and if I live up to that day in and day out."

And for Dungy, it all comes back to how you define excellence. Is it defined by the number of games won or by individual performance? If the former is the case, disappointment is sure to follow. "But excellence is about how you do things and doing the very best you can," Dungy says. "Excellence doesn't mean you always have to win or always have to be in first place."

To maintain that healthy perspective, Dungy says the key is staying focused on Christ. "If you're only focused on excellence in your job or excellence on the field, you will get totally out of balance and out of whack. Yes, I need to be excellent as a coach. I need to be excellent as a Christian. I need to be excellent as a father. I need to be excellent as a person in the community and strive for that excellence everywhere and not just in one area."

That also means never sacrificing integrity for excellence. Although an increasing number of athletes and coaches have succumbed to the temptation to cheat, Dungy can point to another of Jesus's parables found in Matthew 7:24–27 for his inspiration to avoid such lapses in character. The story talks about two men—one who builds his house on the rock and the other who builds his house on the sand. When the rains come, the house built on the rock stands firm while the house built on sand crumbles to the ground.

That vivid imagery illustrates what happens to those who heed God's call to competitive integrity versus those who cut corners and look for a quick fix on their route to success. The latter cannot be legitimately equated with godly excellence.

"You have to look at excellence in every way," Dungy says. "I have to be excellent in my integrity, not just excellent in winning. If I'm just trying to be excellent in winning, that can lead to some problems.

We are bound by rules, and we are not going to cheat or do certain things to win, but that is still the goal—to be excellent. And there is nothing wrong with that. As Christians, it is great to be able to show the world that, yes, we can do it the Lord's way, but we can be excellent while we do it."

And according to 1 Chronicles 4:9–10, striving for excellence can have a tangible result. Jabez, a man referred to in verse 9 as "more honorable than his brothers," unabashedly made his desire known to God. In verse 10, Jabez says, "If only You would bless me, extend my border, let Your hand be with me, and keep me from harm, so that I will not cause any pain." That same verse concludes by telling us that "God granted his request."

While the end result may be different for each individual—based on God's purpose for his or her life—ultimately excellence can be wrapped up by what Paul wrote in 2 Timothy 4:7: "I have fought the good fight, I have finished the race, I have kept the faith" and 1 Corinthians 9:24, the Scripture that so impressed Dungy: "Do you not know that the runners in a stadium all race, but only one receives the prize? Run in such a way to win the prize." Both passages allude to the "big win" that is yet to be awarded in heaven.

"I talk about excellence a lot, because I think from a Christian perspective, that can get lost sometimes," Dungy says. "We talk so much about how it's 'just God's will' and that we want to serve Him, but He wants us to be excellent in what we do. He's placed us in our careers. We all run to receive a prize and to win. I never want to forget that part of it. We should run to win."

Training Time

1. For Tony Dungy and other NFL coaches, the "big win" can be equated with a victory in the

Super Bowl. What does the "big win" mean for you in your life?

2. What are some of the characteristics that Dungy's NFL peers say have contributed to his excellent results both on and off the field? How do you think your peers would describe your pursuit of excellence? What characteristics would you like to see increased in your life so that excellence would be possible?

3. Read 1 Corinthians 9:24–27. As a follower of Christ, what do you think it means to "win the prize"? What are some examples of crowns that will not last? What is your concept of a crown that will last forever?

4. Read Luke 12:13–21. What different types of people in modern society does the rich man in this parable represent? What are the dangers of resting, or taking it easy, after achieving varying degrees of success? What

message about excellence do you think Jesus is trying to tell us through this parable?

5. Read 2 Timothy 4:1–8. What are some things Paul says we will have to endure? How does having the proper perspective on winning and losing while we are in the midst of pursuing excellence help us deal with such challenges?

journal

2

Free to Play
with Passion

LAUREN HOLIDAY
US Women's National Soccer Team

Therefore, brothers, by the mercies of God, I urge you to present your bodies as a living sacrifice, holy and pleasing to God; this is your spiritual worship.

Romans 12:1

This is the will of God for you: your freedom. Uncompromising, unrelenting, indomitable freedom. For this Christ died. For this he rose. For this he sent his Spirit. There is nothing he wills with more intensity under the glory of his own name than this: your freedom.

John Piper

Lauren Holiday can't remember a time when a soccer ball hasn't been within her foot's reach. Thanks to her older brother Aaron's influence, she fell in love with the game at an early age even though her home state of Indiana is more known for basketball. Holiday (*née* Cheney) played that sport too, but nothing quite compared to the feeling of kicking the ball around and sending it whizzing past her opponent's goal-keeper.

"I played with the boys until I was twelve years old," she says. "I just loved soccer and had a passion for it."

Holiday's enthusiasm reached a fevered pitch in 1999 with the rise of the United States Women's National Team at the World Cup. That's when she realized just how badly she wanted to play for her country. In that moment, Holiday was convinced she would play on that same international stage one day.

"I especially liked watching Michelle Akers," she recalls. "She always worked hard and she played center midfielder, the same position that I played. Her work ethic and her strength were so evident. I really admired that."

Holiday was also introduced to the Christian faith at a young age, but didn't develop the same fervor in church as she had experienced on the field. That began to change in junior high school when she went to some youth camps and started to discover the presence of God. Then in high school, Holiday made the Under-20 Women's National Team along with Tobin Heath and several other Christian athletes. But it was head coach Tim Schultz's influence that made the biggest difference.

"He was on fire for the Lord," Holiday says. "I remember praying one night, 'God, I want what he has.' He was so passionate about his faith and I wanted that too. And that's when I really started to seek the Lord."

Holiday's newfound passion was both challenged and fortified when she left the Midwest to play collegiately at UCLA.

The culture shock hit her hard. There were only a handful of Christians on the team. Not surprisingly, many of her teammates simply wanted to be a part of the Hollywood scene. Holiday had to learn that the value of her actions and her witness sometimes mattered more than her ability to evangelize with her words. But those upperclassmen who shared the same faith also provided comfort, encouragement, and fellowship.

"They were involved in church and they just swept me up and included me in a routine that included regular Sunday service attendance and weekly Bible studies," Holiday explains. "I was immersed in nondenominational Christian churches and experienced worship for the first time like I had never experienced it before."

Holiday also excelled on the soccer field, where she became the first UCLA women's player to become a four-time First-Team All-American. That success eventually helped her earn a spot on the

US Women's National Team. She made her first appearance on January 26, 2007, against Germany, and scored her first goal against Mexico less than four months later. When Abby Wambach broke her leg in 2008, Holiday filled the open roster spot for the 2008 Olympic Games in Beijing.

By 2010, she had risen from the bench to take a starting role on the team. Holiday was also getting more comfortable living out her faith in an environment that included many divergent philosophies.

"It completely brought me out of my comfort zone to be around people that didn't believe in the same thing," she says. "Playing at UCLA definitely prepared me for that experience. I learned to love people unconditionally no matter what they believe in. Being with the national team has allowed me to just love on people and be salt and light."

As Holiday's star continued to rise, she found more opportunities to utilize her newfound platform. Fellowship of Christian Athletes was one of those outlets. Holiday, who attended a Huddle group and numerous FCA events in high school, believes that she has a special message to share with the next generation.

"I have a passion to let kids know that sports and God don't have to be separate," she says. "God gave them their talents and He's given them this pedestal for a reason. They don't have to choose between being great at their sport and following Jesus. It's encouraging to be able to speak truth into their lives, especially at such an impressionable young age."

In those moments, it all comes together for Holiday, who can now see the spiritual progression that's taken place over the course of more than a decade. As she has become more passionate about Jesus, she has likewise become even more passionate about soccer—not because of the accolades, the recognition, or even the increasing ability to use her status to build His kingdom. Her passion is ignited because of the freedom she has found in her relationship with Christ.

"Sometimes that can be the hardest part," Holiday says. "I haven't always been able to play freely, to play with no pressure."

That's why Romans 12:1 is one of her favorite Bible verses: "Therefore, brothers, by the mercies of God, I urge you to present your bodies as a living sacrifice, holy and pleasing to God; this is your spiritual worship."

"I try to think about that every time I play," Holiday adds. "At the 2011 World Cup, I was playing in the biggest tournament of my life. I was playing an unfamiliar position. I remember thinking, 'Lord, this is my act of worship.' It can still be a struggle at times, but I always try to keep in mind that He gave me this talent. This isn't for me. This is for Him. That gives me so much joy."

Along the way, Holiday has been blessed with some teammates who are likewise playing passionately in the freedom that only comes from Heaven. Tobin Heath, Amy Rodriguez, and Heather O'Reilly are just a few of the players that have stuck together over the past several years and organized Bible studies, Sunday services, and prayer gatherings.

"I've grown up with Tobin," Holiday says. "I've played with her for years. She has such a recklessness for Jesus. Watching her has set me on fire, and she's done that for the other believers on the team. It's awesome to have so many women going through the same struggles that can talk to each other about it. Without other believers on the team, it would be a much more difficult job."

Her newest passion is her relationship with NBA point guard Jrue Holiday. The two met at UCLA and were married in 2013. Not only do the two share a love for both Christ and sports, they are also vigilant in keeping each other accountable to living in freedom and allowing their light to shine through the way they conduct themselves while playing at a high level and while living out their marriage on a very public stage.

"It's a hard lifestyle to keep Christ first," Holiday admits. "But it's so important to be vocal about it. It's important for me to show girls that you can be a woman of God. It's important for Jrue to show guys that you can be a man of God. To do that, we always try to make sure that He is prevalent in our lives. God is the only reason that we're able to have the relationship that we have. We always tell each other that we're going to be different."

Holiday never wants to go back to living under the weight of performance. Instead, she desires to pursue godly excellence in everything she does. Over time, Holiday has come to understand the power in these words that the apostle Paul penned to the believers in Galatia: "Christ has liberated us to be free. Stand firm then and don't submit again to the yoke of slavery" (Gal. 5:1).

"There's so much passion and joy in the freedom that only He can give," Holiday says. "That's why I need to be more proactive in following the Spirit every day. I first encountered and accepted how alive the Holy Spirit could be in my life and the lives around me when I was in college. I've been growing in that ever since. True freedom only comes when we allow Him to work in us and through us. I can't imagine life without it."

Training Time

1. What are some things that you are passionate about?

2. Have you ever felt stress or pressure while doing something you loved? Explain.

3. What are some things that you would identify as your spiritual acts of worship?

4. What do you think is the correlation between passion and freedom? Have you personally experienced this in your life?

5. Go back and read Galatians 5:1. Do you feel like you're living in God's freedom? If not, what are some things you can do today to help you start living a more free and passionate life in Christ?

journal

journal

3

Good Habits

ALBERT PUJOLS
MLB First Baseman and Three-Time National League MVP

Therefore, my dear brothers, be steadfast, immovable, always excelling in the Lord's work, knowing that your labor in the Lord is not in vain.

1 Corinthians 15:58

We are what we repeatedly do. Excellence, then, is not an act, but a habit.

Aristotle

Numbers. In sports, they often mean everything. Even numbers that seem inconsequential can spell the difference between winning and losing—the difference between a gold medal and a silver medal, the difference between a championship and second place, the difference between greatness and mediocrity.

Numbers are especially important to professional athletes because things such as a league-leading scoring average or a consistent number of home runs can result in high-dollar contracts and job security.

But strangely, Albert Pujols (whose career numbers are eye-popping even to the average sports fan) could not care less about his batting average, his RBI totals or his on-base percentage.

"My goals every day are to help my team win and hopefully have the opportunity to go to the playoffs or the World Series," Pujols says. "That's my goal every year—to win the World Series. Through Christ, I get to please people through that because that's what we play for. God has blessed me to win a World Series in such a young career. After my first seven years in the big leagues, playing in two World Series and six playoffs was just unbelievable. It was more than I could ask for. But I really make sure I keep my eyes on Christ first. If I do that, I think everything else will be easy."

For Pujols, growing up in a poor family in the Dominican Republic was anything but easy. He did what he could to help by taking odd jobs here and there, but Pujols mostly tried his best to work hard in school and stay out of trouble by playing baseball every afternoon in the streets. His family moved to the United States in the early 1990s and eventually settled in the Kansas City area. Pujols excelled in baseball at Fort Osage High School in Independence, Missouri, where he was a two-time All-State selection. He then played college ball at Maple Woods Community College, where one season was enough to attract the attention of some Major League clubs.

Pujols was drafted by the St. Louis Cardinals in the thirteenth round of the 1999 draft, but he turned down a meager signing bonus and played that season in the Jayhawk League in Kansas. A year later, he was in the Cardinals' fold and headed to the minor leagues, where he spent most of the 2000 season playing for the team's single-A club in Peoria. When Pujols started spring training in 2001, the Cardinals began to look for a way to include him on their 25-man roster. Once he took to the field that season, it became evident to all that Pujols would be a force to contend with for years to come.

But his Major League debut on April 2, 2001, is not even close to being the most important day in Pujols's life. That day had arrived three years earlier when he met his future wife, Deidre, a born-again Christian who invited him to church. Before that, Pujols had limited knowledge of the Bible and knew little more than the fact that "there was a guy who died for us."

He began attending a Bible study with Deidre at Kansas City Baptist Temple. As God softened his heart, Pujols's desire for a relationship with the Creator slowly grew until he could no longer resist. "There were times when I really wanted [to commit my life to Christ], but I never got a person to push me like my wife [did]," Pujols says. "It's like a lot of people believe it, but they don't want to get saved—they don't think they're ready. I think that day I was ready. I told my wife that when I walked into church that day, I was going to get saved."

Early on, Pujols called on Christian teammates such as Andy Benes, Mike Matheny, and J. D. Drew for accountability and spiritual mentoring. Now, years later, Pujols is the one taking the role he once relied upon so heavily.

"I'm growing in the Word right now, and God is showing me things," Pujols says. "If I hadn't accepted Christ when I first starting playing baseball, I don't know where I would be right now. It wasn't like I was a bad little boy. I never drank. I never smoked. I don't party. I don't do all of those things that people think you have to do to have fun in this life. There are other things that you can do to have fun in this world. People think that they need to go out and have a glass of wine or drink and all of that, but to me it's not important. I can have fun just going to the park and spending time with my family. I get to come home after a tough night at a stadium and see my kids laughing and spend time with them. That's more important to me."

Pujols's relationship with Christ has not only made him a better husband and father but it has also helped strengthen him in his lifelong pursuit of excellence, a concept that he defines as "just doing the best that I can with what I do and then honoring God."

He was first inspired to strive for excellence when he was still in the Dominican Republic, initially by his large family and then later by the many professional baseball players who have emerged from his home country. Here in the United States,

Pujols credits his wife, Deidre, for teaching him even more about excellence—specifically, excellence as it relates to the Word of God.

Rick Horton had a front-row seat to Pujols's ten years in St. Louis. Horton, a former Cardinals pitcher, is a member of the club's broadcast team and also serves as the area director for Fellowship of Christian Athletes. He describes Pujols as "a miraculous athlete" with "incredible drive and determination." And he believes that Pujols's good habits—preparation, focus, and discipline—separate him from the rest of the players.

"His preparation is beyond what most Major League Baseball players do," Horton says. "He really studies the film, and he's good at it. He studies the film of his opponents. He knows and understands the swing and breaks down the swing. He also hits more baseballs off the tee when nobody is looking than most players do. He really works at his craft. He's got a great work ethic. In all of the hoopla that's surrounded him over the years, he doesn't back down on his work. He just works harder. Every year going into spring training, he always says he's just trying to make the team; and everybody laughs when he says it because he's one of the best hitters on the planet, but at some deep level, he really means that."

Pujols literally takes nothing for granted. It doesn't matter to him that he won the 2001 National League (NL) Rookie of the Year award. It doesn't matter to him that he was named NL Most Valuable Player in 2005, 2008, and 2009. It doesn't matter to him that he has one of the top four highest career batting averages among active players. It doesn't matter to him that he's made nine appearances in the All-Star Game. It doesn't matter to him how many awards and big numbers he puts up. Pujols still approaches each season the same.

"Without preparation, you won't have excellence," Pujols says. "So I really try to prepare myself in the off-season for three months. I work hard in the gym and try to keep myself healthy. After you've laid the bat and glove down for three months, you can't just show up to spring training and expect to have excellence. It's impossible."

Horton believes that Pujols's consistent training is even more amazing considering the year-round demands on his time. "He's always at the park early," he says. "He's always doing something valuable. You never see him wasting time. He's also pretty focused. When he gets to the park, he goes about his business. Now he's got more business than everybody else does. A lot of players can't handle being the superstar. You're the team spokesman. Everybody wants to interview you. Players from the other team send you over a box of things to sign. It really does happen. I saw [Mark] McGwire go through that.

It's unbelievable. But Pujols is impervious to distraction."

Pujols admits that it is very tough to stay focused. "There are a lot of distractions out there in this world right now," Pujols says. "There's women, drugs—everything. If you open the newspaper right now, you can see that every day there's something happening in this world. It's tough. I make sure that all of that doesn't get into my mind. I'm here to try to serve God and to try to honor Him and not get caught up in those distractions. Am I perfect?

"No. I just try to stay focused and make sure that whatever I do is to honor God. So those distractions are easy for me to avoid."

Preparation and focus, however, mean nothing without rock-solid discipline that is fortified by the will to succeed and to be excellent. Horton says that Pujols has stayed disciplined by establishing boundaries even when they can sometimes bring criticisms from those who don't understand (or respect) his need to stay true to specific training routines that provide mental, physical, and spiritual balance.

"Albert's got pretty thick skin," Horton says. "He's totally immune to that. He knows who he is. He's comfortable with who he is. He's comfortable in his relationship with Christ, and he's doing what he can to grow personally and to lead others. He has had numerous occasions where he's presented his faith to his teammates and he knows he's accountable for that, but he's not trying to please men. I think that's helped him say no when he needed to say no and say yes when he needed to say yes."

As Pujols's spiritual life has grown exponentially, so has his understanding of the purpose for excellence on the baseball field, which also blends into his personal life, where his ability to impact others is just as significant.

"Now I live for Christ where before I was thinking about myself," Pujols says. "I've been saved since 1999, and I've seen how Christ has changed my life—how God has worked in my life and in my family. I see changed lives through [our Pujols Family Foundation] every day because God has given me the opportunity when before it was all about Albert Pujols. Now, through Christ, He has shown me that it's not about Albert Pujols. It's about Him. It's about helping others. I just thank God for allowing me to call on Him and for being my Father and for sending Jesus to die on the cross for my sins and for giving me the opportunity to leave that selfishness I had in the past and to live for Him right now."

Furthermore, Pujols contends that because of his daily commitment to excellence, he now has the opportunity to share the message of salvation through Christ with others—teammates, team administrators, and fans—who otherwise would not be as receptive to him.

"You have to set an example of excellence," Pujols says. "If you were the average guy and you go out there and don't take care of your business and you don't do the things you're supposed to do and you don't lead by example—which is what God wants us to do—you're not going to have the opportunity to witness. If they see me doing crazy things, they're going to say, 'What are you talking about? You're just doing the same things that I'm doing.' But I have to set an example in the clubhouse. I'm not perfect. The only One who was perfect was Christ. We want to be perfect. We want to be like Him, but that's impossible because if we were perfect, we wouldn't be here right now."

Pujols has used his platform as a star player to influence his teammates in both St. Louis and now Los Angeles, where he plays for the Angels and shares the hope of eternal life with them.

"I have a really good relationship with Yadier [Molina]," he says. "I thank God that He gave me the opportunity to witness to him, and he gave his life to Christ. To me, that's bigger than hitting a home run in game seven of the World Series with two outs in the bottom of the ninth. That was the best thing that happened to me that year—knowing that I witnessed to one of my teammates, a guy who I really admire and a guy who I really tried to help."

Pujols also displays his commitment to excellence off the field through the Pujols Family Foundation, which he runs with his wife. They work to support families touched by Down syndrome, in part due to the fact that his adopted daughter, Isabella (born to Deidre prior to their marriage in 2000), was born with the condition. Through the foundation, the Pujols family also actively supports many programs aimed at improving the education, economic situation, and physical environment of impoverished children and their families in the Dominican Republic. He and his wife also make an annual medical missions trip to his native country during the off-season.

"Knowing the Word of God and going back to the Dominican Republic, I'm able to teach people about what God has done in my life, and I'm able to set an example and show them who I live for," Pujols says. "Christ is using me through the foundation, so I can witness to people who don't know the Word. They listen because I'm Albert Pujols the baseball player. Well, it's not about Albert Pujols. It's about Christ. Every day I thank God for that. He could have picked anyone, but I'm grateful and thankful that He's using me to reach these poor kids in the Dominican Republic who don't have anything."

"[Pujols] talks a lot about his responsibility to do his best with the gifts God has given him," Horton adds. "He says that publicly all the time. I think he's got a really good understanding of stewardship. We always think about that as a financial thing, but it's primarily a giftedness issue. He uses his gifts and his finances. I think that's part of his spiritual growth that keeps him connected. He's also growing in his leadership."

That's just another reason why Pujols believes excellence has little to do with numbers and everything to do with giving all you have to the glory of God. His philosophy can be traced back to Hebrews 13:15–16, which says, "Therefore, through Him let us continually offer up to God a sacrifice of praise, that is, the fruit of our lips that confess His name. Don't neglect to do good and to share, for God is pleased with such sacrifices."

"I haven't done anything to deserve what God has given me," Pujols says. "I really enjoy my relationship with Him and I enjoy my family and I enjoy this game. I'm having fun with this game.

This is a platform that He has given me, so I can glorify Him and I can witness to other people. I make sure that I do my 110 percent and do my best to honor Him."

Training Time

1. Numbers have an important place in athletics and other areas of life. What are some ways that numbers impact the difference between success and failure in your life? How closely do you keep up with your numbers? Does the way you approach statistical information help or hinder your performance?

2. For Pujols, the pursuit of excellence starts with preparation. What are some ways that you prepare for competition? Read Ephesians 6:10–18. How is a soldier's preparation similar to that of a competitor? What are some consequences of being unprepared?

3. Read 1 Corinthians 15:58. What are some distractions you deal with on a daily basis? How does Paul encourage us to avoid such distractions? What do you think "your labor in the Lord is not in vain" means?

4. Read Proverbs 21:31. What motivates you to have good habits as an athlete? What about in other areas of your life? How disappointed are you when you don't win or don't achieve your goals? How does the passage in Proverbs keep performance results in perspective?

5. Read Hebrews 13:15–16. In what ways are good habits "a sacrifice of praise" (v. 15)? How does placing God at the top of your priority list keep you focused on striving for excellence?

journal

4

Pushing Through

JEAN DRISCOLL
*Former Olympic and
Paralympic Wheelchair Athlete*

Rejoice in hope; be patient in affliction; be persistent in prayer.

Romans 12:12

Persistence is the twin sister of excellence. One is a matter of quality; the other, a matter of time.

Marabel Morgan

When Jean Driscoll was a teenager, she had all of the same negative ideas about wheelchairs as everyone else. They were cumbersome and limiting, and using one meant the end of any shot at a normal life. And that's exactly how she felt when, as a high school sophomore, she was forced to use one herself.

"I thought my life was over," Driscoll candidly says.

It took another ten to fifteen years for Driscoll, whose condition was caused by spina bifida, to learn that her life was in fact *not* over. It was just beginning. And then in 2002 at a Bible study, she stumbled across Daniel 7:9—a passage that confirmed what God had been revealing to her all along: "As I kept watching, thrones were set in place, and the Ancient of Days took His seat. His clothing was white like snow, and the hair of His head like whitest wool. His throne was flaming fire; its wheels were blazing fire."

By then, Driscoll had already come to understand the purpose behind her disability. Many years of life experience and spiritual growth separated her from the pain, hurt, and confusion that surrounded her childhood and teenage years. But that didn't make her discovery any less inspiring.

"Daniel is giving a description of God," Driscoll explains. "It says that there are wheels on His throne, and then

it says there's fire coming out from behind it. Not only does God's throne have
wheels, He burns rubber! Anytime I've
had an opportunity to talk with people
who use wheelchairs and feel bad about
being in a chair, I tell them, 'Not only
are you made in the image of God, but
your wheelchair is made in the image of
His throne!'"

When Driscoll was growing up in Mil-
waukee, Wisconsin, there was no one
around to give her that same kind of encouragement. At the time of her birth in
1966, nearly half of the babies born with
spina bifida (a birth defect that results in
improper development of the spine) died
due to infection or some other complica-
tion. Even though her case was relatively
mild, she still needed to wear leg braces,
and she struggled with balance.

"My feet turned out to the side, and
I would sway back and forth," Driscoll
says. "Because I walked so awkwardly, I
got stared at a lot. I got teased a lot. So I

grew up not having good self-esteem and not feeling good about myself. I always felt frustrated because my body didn't work like everybody else's. I would try to be involved in different sports activities, but my legs were not strong enough. So I was the scorekeeper for our grade-school volleyball team, and I was the manager of the girl's basketball team, but I never really got to get in there and get dirty."

Driscoll dealt with her challenges as best as she could under the circumstances. But in the 1970s, there was still a long way to go in terms of technological advancements and public support for people with disabilities. Unfortunately, Driscoll's life became even more difficult during her freshman year at high school when she crashed her newly acquired bicycle on the way home from a babysitting job. Driscoll took a hard fall, and because of her weak lower-body muscles, she dislocated her hip. That tragic mishap led to five major operations over the next year and required her to wear a body cast that covered three-fourths of her body.

"It was a really long year. I spent a lot of time by myself," Driscoll says. "I remember praying over and over and over again that maybe after all of these surgeries were over, my feet would point forward instead of out to the side and it would be one more way that I would be like everybody else. I just wanted to be like everybody else. That was my goal. I wanted to blend in. I hated sticking out."

She was sent home to recover and work on flexibility, but over the course of two weeks, her hip again became dislocated. None of the surgeries had worked and now came the inevitable: first crutches and eventually the dreaded wheelchair.

"I was so mad at God because I thought that He was picking on me," Driscoll says. "First, I was born with this disability and I was constantly teased, and then I had all of these painful surgeries. I've got foot-long scars over both hips. None of those surgeries worked, and doctors are supposed to be able to fix everything. I didn't understand why they couldn't fix my body. It was really a hard time."

But Driscoll had no idea that God would use the wheelchair and her disability to open doors to some incredible and unimaginable places. Her journey began as a high-school junior when she met a young man who also had spina bifida and used a wheelchair. He invited Driscoll to play wheelchair soccer, which was one of many adapted sports that were becoming increasingly popular with people who used wheelchairs.

With an array of stereotypes dominating her mind, Driscoll wanted no part of what she assumed was an inferior knockoff of the real deal. However, she eventually did go to observe a practice, where she was surprised at the intense and fierce competition she saw. Driscoll's instant intrigue led her to discover a wide range of wheelchair sports, including ice

hockey, football, softball, tennis, and basketball. It was the last, wheelchair basketball, which brought her to the University
of Illinois—a move that she says changed
her life.

Driscoll was at home one day when she
saw the women's 800-meter wheelchair
race at the 1984 Summer Olympics in Los
Angeles being broadcast live on television.
Her family didn't watch sports much, but
somehow she was walking by the television, on her crutches, just as Sharon Hed-
rick won that historic race. Driscoll was
captivated by it all but still had no idea
that she would soon be heading down the
same path. Then she was recruited to play
wheelchair basketball by the University of
Illinois, where her coach was Brad Hed-
rick, the husband of the woman Driscoll
had watched make Olympic history by
winning the first Olympic gold medal
awarded to a wheelchair athlete.

At Illinois, Driscoll added track and
road racing to her collegiate repertoire.

That's where she began working with another key figure in her life—Marty Morse,
coach of the University of Illinois wheelchair track and field team. After a string
of successful road races that ranged from
5K to 12K, Morse tried to talk Driscoll
into competing in a marathon. Initially,
she was fearful of the distance and had
no desire to do so. But she finally gave
in and raced at the Chicago Marathon.
Driscoll's surprising second-place finish
qualified her for the prestigious Boston
Marathon, although she again wasn't ter-
ribly thrilled at the idea of racing such a
long distance.

From there, however, her competitive
life took flight. She not only won the
1990 Boston Marathon but also broke
the world record. Driscoll went on to win
seven consecutive Boston Marathons and
an eighth race in 2000. She set new world
marks a total of five times.

Driscoll also found great success at the
Olympic Games, where she won silver in

the 800-meter Women's Wheelchair Exhibition Event at the 1992 and 1996 Olympics in Barcelona and Atlanta. From 1988 to 2000, she competed in four consecutive Paralympic Games and won a total of five gold medals, three silver medals, and four bronze medals.

In the early years of her transformation, Driscoll still struggled with identity and purpose. Her understanding of God was skewed by tragedy and tumult. "I always felt like I was being punished because God was a big, mad God and if you did things wrong, He was going to get you," Driscoll says. "My question was, why is He only calling me out? Why isn't He ever mad at my siblings?"

As Driscoll's legend grew, so did her relationship with some people whom God was placing in her life. An athletic administrator at Illinois named Debbie Richardson was one key individual who invited her to church and introduced her to Fellowship of Christian Athletes. It was a slow process for Driscoll, but by the time she had won her third Boston Marathon in 1992, she finally started to acknowledge God's part in all of it.

"I started to see a God who wasn't constantly judgmental, constantly angry, constantly punishing me," Driscoll says. "It broke those chains on my heart. It was such a freeing experience."

When Driscoll surrendered her heart and her life to Christ, the passionate pursuit of excellence came into clearer focus. She had always defined excellence as "giving your all" but now understood for whom her excellence was truly intended.

"In 1992, I started looking back, and it was a very short racing career to that point; but the success that I had experienced was phenomenal," Driscoll says. "I started looking at things that God had placed in my life. I started to see my disability more in terms of a workout and training. When I was younger and able to walk, it took all the energy I had. I would be exhausted after even short distances, but it helped me develop other areas in my life like mental toughness and never quitting, because I was always trying to keep up with everybody else."

Later on in her spiritual journey, Driscoll was writing down her thoughts for a speech at a Christian organization and came to an even deeper realization of God's plan for her life. "All of those early years when I was being picked on and I thought that God was picking on me, I was so tired of being picked on," Driscoll says. "Then I realized that I had been picked *out*. I had been picked out to do things that God created only me to do. I was working so hard to blend in and be like everybody else, and He kept pulling me out and showing me that I wasn't like everybody else. My life was not meant to blend in, but it was meant to stand out. That just blew me away—and it still does."

As Driscoll grew in her faith, she began to understand the correlation between the

Bible and her growing physical and mental strength. Romans 12:12 has been a particularly inspirational Scripture in her quest for excellence: "Rejoice in hope; be patient in affliction; be persistent in prayer."

"Perseverance has been one of those things at my core," Driscoll says. "It took me two or three times the effort to do what everyone else was doing. That has stuck with me throughout my life. It's one of those things that God was cultivating in me without my even realizing it. So as I have moved through different experiences of life and different seasons of life, certainly athletics was huge and still is such a part of my success story, but perseverance had everything to do with my ability to get through those workouts, whether I was feeling strong or whether I was feeling weak."

Personal experience has revealed another truth to Driscoll: excellence requires some level of perseverance, and perseverance is ultimately fueled by hope.

"I don't think you can have excellence without perseverance," she says. "I think the two things work together. There are other qualities that are folded in that too. Hope has a lot to do with perseverance. The Bible tells us that the greatest gifts are faith, hope, and love, with love being the greatest—but hope is huge. Hope is what makes or breaks people. You can't persevere without having that hope of what's to come."

But perseverance isn't just a matter of stiffening one's neck and bulldozing through adversity. Driscoll says there are a number of hindrances to perseverance that make it all too easy for people to give up on themselves.

"I believe our biggest limitations are the ones that we place on ourselves or the ones that we allow others to place on us," Driscoll says. "So often people are told you can't do this and you can't do that. Growing up with a disability, you constantly hear people putting you down.

When people place limitations and negative talk on others, it can be a huge hindrance. But also our own negative talk and our own self-imposed limitations keep us from doing things."

It's hard to say which is the greater tragedy: people who raise the white flag and fail to see their dreams through or people who persevere but then take the credit and refuse to acknowledge God throughout the process. Driscoll believes that the latter is usually motivated by the insecurity that results from emptiness, sadness, and loneliness. On the flip side, it's those who readily seek help and cry out in their time of need who often find a portal to divine strength and grace.

"There's a freedom in being able to reach out to others in your own weakness," Driscoll says. "That's exactly what God calls us to do. He wants us to bring our weakness. He wants us to come to Him, and He will give us strength. He is the gift of life. So you don't have to rely on yourself. It doesn't take as much energy to get through life, and you have a brighter perspective."

Driscoll has learned all of these things as part of her own lifelong journey from physical brokenness to spiritual wholeness. She readily shares the message of hope with all who will listen, but her story has proven especially powerful to disabled individuals in such developing countries as Ghana, where Raphael Nkegbe and Ajara Busanga are among those whose lives Driscoll has touched.

"That's the gift that I'm able to give to those people with disabilities in Africa right now," she says. "In many parts of Africa, individuals with disabilities are seen as being cursed by God. They have no value. They're considered to be like the dogs that run around on the ground. It's so opposite of what the Bible says."

Driscoll made her first trip to Ghana in 2001. She introduced wheelchair racing to Nkegbe and Busanga, who have since developed into world-class athletes. Both of them competed at the 2004 Paralympics in Athens, and Busanga won a gold medal at the 2008 All Africa Games. More importantly, both of them went from being outcasts to receiving celebrity treatment in their home country.

And none of this would have been possible had Driscoll not persevered and continued to strive for excellence in every facet of her life.

"God has given me a platform that reaches other continents," Driscoll says. "I couldn't even walk a block to my own school. It's tremendously humbling to think that God trusts me with all of this. What an incredible honor—and what joy."

Training Time

1. What are some personal challenges or physical limitations that you have dealt with? Did you ever feel like

giving up? What was it that gave you the strength to fight through those times?

2. Jean Driscoll had several people in her life who pushed her to achieve great things—even when she didn't believe in herself. Who are some people who have been encouragers throughout your career and your life in general? In what ways did they give you support and inspiration? When have you been able to fill that role for someone else?

3. Driscoll says that her disability helped her to develop mental toughness. What does mental toughness mean to you? Do you consider yourself mentally tough? If so, what has helped you develop that quality?

4. Read Romans 12:12. What do you think it means to "be patient in affliction"? In what ways do your trials push you to excellence? What are some trying circumstances you've

faced in your life that forced you to be patient? How did dealing with those situations impact your ability to handle any challenges that followed?

5. Read John 17:4. In what ways did Jesus persevere in order to bring glory to God? What are some ways that you can glorify God through perseverance?

journal

5

A Better Representative of God

Roy Helu Jr.

NFL Running Back

Whatever you do, do it enthusiastically, as something done for the Lord and not for men, knowing that you will receive the reward of an inheritance from the Lord. You serve the Lord Christ.

Colossians 3:23–24

Any goal that causes you to love God more brings glory to God. Any goal you set that causes you to trust God more brings glory to God. Any goal you set that causes to you obey God, to love God, to serve God brings glory to God.

Rick Warren

Roy Helu Jr. has understood the concept of athletic excellence since his days as a star prep athlete at San Ramon Valley

(CA) High School, where he earned All-East Bay League honors and rushed for over 2,500 combined yards as a junior and senior.

But it wasn't until his senior year at the University of Nebraska that he really began to grasp the true purpose behind giving his best on the football field. Ironically, it wasn't something he discovered while playing for the legendary Cornhusker program, but it was instead the lessons he learned while dealing with some adversity throughout his sophomore and junior years.

"It's one thing to hear people talk about injuries, but when you experience it, it's totally different," Helu says. "I actually appreciated all the tough times I went through at Nebraska because you look back and say, 'Wow! I've experienced things that are even harder than this and I came out on the other side of it.'"

One of the tougher moments came in a home game against Texas Tech where

Helu hurt the acromioclavicular (AC) joint in his shoulder. The injury limited his ability to contribute for the next two games and ultimately impeded his impact on Nebraska's Holiday Bowl victory against Arizona. The downtime turned out to be a blessing in disguise.

"Up until that point, even going back to when I was little, I thought that football was it," Helu admits. "That's what life was all about. I found my happiness and joy in it and it would alter my mentality. When I got hurt and I wasn't playing as well, after the season I looked back and I was like, 'This can't be it. This football thing can't be the highlight of my life.'"

Helu took the opportunity to get deeper into God's Word. He had already been attending a Bible study group, dating back to his freshman year. But now, it was more than just a thing to do in a small college town like Lincoln. Helu was ready to dig in and discover his true purpose.

"From then on, God showed me a whole lot of stuff," he says. "During the injury, days were really hard. One day would feel like a week. You had to be mentally tough and God provided me with strength. I didn't have enough strength on my own to get through that. I'm thankful for the hard times. They built up the character in my heart that I continue to rely on when things get even harder. That's when I can look back and see what God has done for me."

Ironically, Helu had already started to learn what it meant to pursue excellence as a Christian. He just hadn't translated it to the field of play. His testimony of faith started back in high school thanks to his mother's spiritual transformation.

"Before I came to college, I knew about God and I postured myself as a Christian," Helu says. "A lot of it just had to do with me behaving good. But behavior modification would only last for so long. And then I remember going to church because my mom went to church. She was reborn during my sophomore year in high school and she started taking me. She wanted me to go to church because she knew I'd be going to college soon. That was her wish for me. So I'd go and I'd be on this spiritual high and think I was going to go back to school and I'd be way different and people would see that. I was just trying to change how I acted because it felt good on Sundays. That would only last for so long until the following Monday, and then I'd start to act out of what was really in my heart and that was nothing but selfish desires."

When Helu arrived in Lincoln for his freshman year, his mother called the team chaplain and asked for him to get in touch with her son. That's what initially led him to the Bible study group. But Helu admits that his life really didn't change much at first until a difficult season and the disbandment of a close friendship drew him into a period of depression and sorrow.

"I just came to the point where I realized life had to be different," he says. "So I called the chaplain and for the first time I was really honest with myself and with people who were really believers. I asked him what it really meant to be a Christian because everyone at that Bible study and in high school were saying they were Christians but their lives didn't look different and neither did mine. He went through Scriptures with me and at that moment I think God called me to His own. I received the Holy Spirit there and I've been on fire ever since."

Along with some new friends, teammates like Prince Amukumara and Eric Hagg, Helu relied heavily on the influence of assistant coaches like Tim Beck and Ron Brown. It was Beck who introduced him to the Max Lucado book *It's Not About Me* and helped him better understand why he played football. Brown was a constant source of wisdom and encouragement as well. During one of those difficult times as a junior, Helu found himself in Brown's office at 6 a.m., before a spring morning practice session, and had a serious talk about life that has stuck with him ever since.

"Roy didn't live or die by football," Brown recalls. "If there's a bright spot in the ministry of Roy Helu, it's that he is a down-to-earth, fun-loving guy who would never take himself so seriously that he became obnoxious to people. He had a humble simplicity to him. He was coachable."

When his senior season rolled around, Helu was finally healthy and ready to put his burgeoning desire for Christ-centered excellence into action. It all came together on October 30, 2010, against Missouri, when he set Nebraska's single-game rushing record with 307 yards on 28 carries including touchdown runs of 73, 66, and 53 yards.

"I didn't have any idea how many yards I had or if it was close to the record,"

Helu says. "Before the game, I was feeling under the weather, but it ended up being an awesome game. Our offensive linemen worked their tails off. I know my name is in the books for rushing over 300 yards, but I hope those guys know that they were a big part of it. After that game, I had a lot of opportunities to share the gospel and give all the glory to God."

That senior season turned out to be the best of his career. He rushed for 1,245 yards and 11 touchdowns, and in the process drew the attention of pro scouts that following spring. The Washington Redskins drafted Helu in the fourth round of the 2011 NFL Draft with the 105th pick. He set a franchise rookie rushing record with three consecutive 100-yard games and the Redskins single-game record against San Francisco with fourteen receptions. Helu was named to the All-Rookie Team that season and spent three more years in Washington before signing a two-year deal with the Oakland Raiders in 2015.

At one point during his time with the Redkins, he told reporters that he wanted to be "a better representative of God on the field" and continue to live out the lessons he had learned during his college days.

"It's about playing every down like it means everything," Helu says. "It means playing with all of my ability and a total release of all of my talents that God has given me. I want to give the same effort on the first play when my body is fresh and wants to get more yards as I do on the 64th play when I'm dragging my feet and my body is telling me that I can't run over a tackler. I pray throughout the game for strength and focus so I can carry out my assignments."

That approach to his career is something that goes back to some of those life-changing conversations he had with Ron Brown at Nebraska.

"Jesus was focused on His mission when He came down and walked among us," Helu says. "People spit in His face. He could have brought angels down. But He was so focused on doing God's will. I try to take on that mentality. I want to be focused on glorifying Him no matter how difficult things might become, but it only comes through knowing God. And I want to know Him a little more every day."

Training Time

1. Besides your relationship with God, what is the one thing that you would say is most important in your life? Have you ever struggled to keep it from being more important than God?

2. Go back and read Colossians 3:23. Do you feel like you have applied that verse to every aspect of your life? If not, what has held you back?

3. Helu had to go through injuries before he could realize that his priorities were out of line. What

adversities have you faced and how
did they impact your perspective on
your priorities?

4. What do you think it might look
   like to be a "better representative
   of God"?

5. What are some things that you can
   start doing today that will help you
   focus on your mission and glorify
   Christ in everything you do?

6

Lasting Legacies

Richard and Kyle Petty

Former NASCAR Drivers

God, You have heard my vows;
You have given a heritage to those
who fear Your name. Add days
to the king's life; may his years
span many generations. May he
sit enthroned before God forever;
appoint faithful love and truth to
guard him. Then I will continually sing of Your name, fulfilling
my vows day by day.

Psalm 61:5–8

The greatest use of life is to
spend it for something that will
outlast it.

William James

Depending on who you're talking to at
the time, conversations about the King
will likely invoke numerous topics. When
it comes to rock and roll, there's no doubt

that immortalized crooner Elvis Presley fits the bill. Then you have the King of Pop, a nickname commonly given to iconic entertainer Michael Jackson.

History has also provided us with numerous real-life kings, including such notable biblical leaders as King David and King Solomon and such well-known English rulers as King James I (known for his commissioning of the King James Version of the Bible) and King Henry VIII (infamously known for his many wives).

But within the world of sports, only one image comes to mind when that nickname is uttered: NASCAR legend Richard Petty.

At six foot two and with the help of his trademark black cowboy hat and boots, Petty towers over most everyone in the garage and can seemingly be seen from half a mile away as he stops to sign autographs for anyone and everyone. His smile, shaded by that recognizable jet-black moustache, is welcoming and sincere. Even though his eyes are hidden by sunglasses, you still get the sense that they are locked in and fully engaged on each and every racing fan who simply wants to get close to greatness.

Robbie Loomis, former vice president of Richard Petty Motorsports, remembers the first time he met the King. At the time, he was working as an engineer with Petty's son, Kyle. (Loomis would eventually spend eleven years at RPM before moving on to Hendrick Motor Sports as the crew chief for Jeff Gordon and then returning to the Pettys in 2006.)

"It was a little bit intimidating," Loomis recalls. "He looked like he was about ten feet tall. But he's such a humble, unassuming, and caring person. He really makes you feel comfortable in any setting."

Kyle Petty jokes that everyone in the shop—himself included—calls Richard the King as well. It's become a matter of habit for most who simply respect the man for his years of excellence, although

Richard Petty still seems a bit uncomfortable with the moniker.

"I don't pay any attention to it," Richard Petty says. "My name's Richard. I've done my thing. I tell them a lot of times, 'It's better to be known as that than some of the stuff people would really like to call you.' They're always calling somebody something."

Richard Petty might have had his fair share of enemies while he was dominating NASCAR throughout the '60s, '70s and '80s, but you wouldn't know that now. Any animosity his opponents once harbored has long since been replaced with praise for the King and his astounding accomplishments.

In a thirty-five-year stock-car racing career that spanned five decades, Petty ran 1,184 races and claimed a record 200 wins, seven Daytona 500 victories, and seven NASCAR Cup titles, a feat that only the late Dale Earnhardt Sr. managed to equal.

Richard Petty was preceded by his father, Lee Petty, who was one of the sport's original stars. In just sixteen years, Lee Petty won fifty-four races and three NASCAR titles (an award that at that time was referred to as the Grand National Championship). Lee Petty also founded Petty Enterprises in 1949—an organization that Richard and Kyle still run today.

NASCAR driver Jeff Green drove the #43 car for the Pettys from 2003 to 2005 and was honored to be part of the legendary team. "There's definitely a lot of heritage there," Green says. "Without Richard and Lee and the whole Petty organization, I don't think our sport would be the same. They laid the foundation. As our sport got bigger and better, it's changed a lot; but without those two hundred victories and the #43 car and however many victories Lee had, I don't think it would be the same sport."

The legacy of excellence that was started by Lee Petty continued with Richard, whose philosophy on the subject is much like the way he raced and the way he continues to do business: straightforward and simple.

"When you get up in the morning, [you ask], *Can I do a little better than I did yesterday?*" he explains. "That's the challenge of not just staying the same. Can we make our business a little bit better? Can we help somebody today who we didn't help yesterday? It's just life."

Richard Petty has likewise passed on that desire to be the best to his son, Kyle, who raced in NASCAR's Cup series from 1979 until 2008. More importantly, he has made a lasting impression on everyone involved in the sport.

"The names Petty and NASCAR go hand in hand," former NASCAR driver Jason Keller says. "I don't think you can think of one without the other really. Richard Petty has done so much for the sport, and Kyle has followed in those footsteps. I've been fortunate enough to do some autograph sessions with Kyle, and it's just amazing how the fans relate to him and how personable he is with the fans. He's no different with the fans than he is with us drivers. I think that's what makes him so real—that he's so personable and you can really relate to him."

Tim Griffin, Motor Racing Outreach's former lead Sprint Cup chaplain, has also been impressed by the Petty family and their contributions to stock-car racing. He often refers to them as "the class of NASCAR," not just because of their commitment to excellence on the track, but also because of how they serve the needs of so many away from the track.

"They're ambassadors of NASCAR," Griffin says. "That's probably the best term for them. They're the class, the standard, both on and off the track. Their desire to elevate the sport with class and dignity is really unparalleled. They've been at it for so long, and they've gained such a high level of professionalism and created so much respect in the community itself. You can't help but respect that."

Kyle Petty has benefited from seeing his father in action as far back as he can remember. He raced for Petty Enterprises from 1979 to 1984 and—following stints with the Wood Brothers and Felix Sabates's Sabco Racing—rejoined the organization in 1997. These days, he has become one of the more popular NASCAR television broadcasters.

Whether it was hanging out in the garage area as an eight-year-old kid or riding in cars owned by his father, Kyle has learned a great deal about excellence, including a personal definition that has taken years of firsthand experience and secondhand observation to craft.

"For me, excellence means always striving to do one's best," he says. "It's pushing past your comfort zone sometimes—not necessarily meeting others' expectations, but meeting God's expectations."

Kyle Petty has wisely taken the advice found in Job 8:8–9, which says, "For ask the previous generation, and pay attention to what their fathers discovered, since we were born only yesterday and know nothing. Our days on earth are but a shadow."

To that end, Petty says he has gleaned many amazing nuggets of wisdom from watching his father in action.

"I've learned to always take the high road," Kyle says. "I've learned to know that God will always serve your needs, even when you aren't sure what your needs may be. He is there. He is with you and helping to guide you to make the right decisions in all aspects of your life. There have certainly been times when we have questioned things that have happened in our lives, but we know that God's strength and power are at work."

In essence, it is the Pettys' faith that is at the crux of their pursuit of excellence. Richard Petty cites his wife, Lynda (who passed away in 2014), as the key to his family's commitment to God, while Kyle Petty mentions his grandmothers Petty and Owens for laying the foundation of faith.

"I don't think you can take your faith in God and put it in a pigeonhole," Kyle says. "It's there all the time, every day, everywhere you're at. It's not something that you put in your pocket, and you bring it out to show people and then put it back up. It's not like a new watch. You need to have it all the time. It shows in not only what you do and how you do it but how you lead your entire life and not just the time you get to stand in front of a TV camera for thirty-two seconds on a Sunday afternoon. That's the time that people see you, and that's the time you use for witnessing. That's a good thing to be able to use.

"But at the same time, it's just as important for that guy that you stop to talk to on the side of the road or someone you're having dinner with and talking to one-on-one," he adds. "You may reach just as many people."

As a testament to his strong faith, Kyle Petty has been a longtime supporter of Motor Racing Outreach, and Tim Griffin always enjoys his weekend visits with Petty—whether it be at Sunday morning chapel service, prerace prayer time, or just a random encounter.

"Before the race, we have the privilege of going to each team as they're on the starting grid before they climb into their car and go out to race," Griffin says. "We pray with each driver. At Michigan one year, I remember Kyle said to me, 'You know, the reason I come to chapel is that I just want to hear the Word. That's what I'm here for. That's what most interests me.'"

In 2000, the Petty family's faith was tested profoundly. On April 5, Lee Petty passed away at the age of 86 after complications from surgery for a stomach aneurysm. While losing a father, grandfather, and great-grandfather was difficult, nothing could prepare the Pettys for the tragedy of May 12. On that day, Kyle Petty's oldest son, Adam, was taking practice laps for the Busch (now Nationwide) Series race at the New Hampshire International Speedway when the throttle in his car stuck and caused him to hit the wall head-on. He was killed instantly.

Adam Petty's death sent shockwaves throughout NASCAR, not just because he was a fellow driver but also because he had become a part of the family. His grandfather Richard Petty says that all of the veteran drivers had known him since he was a child and had adopted him as one of their own.

"When something like that happens, it doesn't only happen to your family, it happens to this entire community," Kyle Petty explains. "This is a community. That's what you've got to keep in mind as well. When you talk about this sport, you've got to remember that we're going to go over there, we're all going to work on our cars, we're all going to go out there on the racetrack and try to beat each other's head in. But after all that's over, we'll come right back over here and, look, we're neighbors with each other."

Prior to his death, Adam Petty had shown great interest in camps that cater to kids with special physical needs and had expressed a desire to help build one near the family headquarters in Level Cross, North Carolina. So when Adam was tragically lost at the age of nineteen, Kyle and his wife, Pattie, decided to fulfill their son's dream.

The result was Victory Junction Gang Camp, which focuses on children with chronic and life-threatening diseases. Richard Petty donated seventy acres of land, and this was followed by donations from many others, including fellow drivers Dale Jarrett, Bobby Labonte, Tony Stewart, Kevin Harvick, Michael Waltrip,

Kurt Busch, Jeff Gordon, and Jimmie Johnson, just to name a few.

Built to look like key elements of a racetrack, the medically safe camp is a place where kids can enjoy simple pleasures such as swimming, bowling, and fishing—things that their conditions would otherwise prevent them from doing. Kyle Petty and his family are constantly raising money to ensure that all campers can attend the camp at no cost.

Victory Junction Gang Camp has become one of the Pettys' great passions. Some have even commented that helping hundreds of kids every year has overtaken the family's desire to win races, although few (if any) would suggest that the competitive fire at RPM has been extinguished. But there is a greater realization from Richard and Kyle that their legacy of excellence is wrapped up in much more than fortune and fame. Instead, they can turn to the Bible for examples of what such a legacy should look like. Proverbs 13:22, for instance, tells us that "a good man leaves an inheritance to his grand-children, but the sinner's wealth is stored up for the righteous."

"To be excellent at what you do is a result of faith," Kyle Petty explains. "Ultimately, we are God's children and are here to serve as disciples of Christ. Always striving for excellence sometimes means forgoing the immediate benefits in exchange for long term."

That sobering thought also brings to mind one of David's prayers found in Psalm 61:5–8:

> God, You have heard my vows; You have given a heritage to those who fear Your name. Add days to the king's life; may his years span many generations. May he sit enthroned before God forever; appoint faithful love and truth to guard him. Then I will continually sing of Your name, fulfilling my vows day by day.

While Richard Petty is already experiencing some of this passage's promise, he rarely stops to think about the legacy of excellence through a lifetime of serving and integrity that he is actively creating for his family and the NASCAR community.

"I haven't really ever gone there," Richard says. "We're doing our thing in our time under our circumstances. Hopefully, you leave a good taste in everybody's mouth, and they remember the good. If something happened to us right now and we're not here anymore, we would hope that you would forget about the racing part and go to the camp, the things that we have left that will enrich other people's lives later down the road where racing won't. Racing will be history and that's what we happened to do, but [the camp] is what we left for the rest of the world."

Kyle Petty wholeheartedly agrees with his father's wise words and has similar thoughts on the subject of legacy. "You're only here 60, 70, 80, 100 years—whatever it is," he says. "In the big picture, you're not here that long. I don't think you need to worry about your legacy. But how do you know that your legacy's not that some kid who has spina bifida or has hemophilia or has AIDS comes to camp and at some point in time 20 or 30 years from now, he has a son or a daughter and tells them about a camp he went to when he was young and then this child grows up and discovers a cure for cancer?"

Tim Griffin has seen the Pettys forge ahead in their quest for excellence and can't help but be inspired by their impeccable vision and unshakable resolve.

"You can't worry about your legacy," he concurs. "It can't be part of your goal. It's a by-product of doing the right thing today. The Pettys have grown to understand that it's an improper focus to have your mind fixed on what people are going to think about you. You've just got to do the right thing that's in front of you today."

As a follower of Christ, Kyle Petty is driven to excellence and understands its ultimate purpose in the grand scheme of life.

"That's simple," he says. "I want to please God. I want Him to know that I believe in Him as my Savior, and because of that, I will do all things to please Him. He has played a large part in my family's life. We are here because of Him. Sure, we question why some things have happened and always will. But it is because of faith that we can pick up and move forward, using those experiences to make us stronger followers of Christ and to strive for excellence in all that we do."

Training Time

1. If there were a poll taken among your family, friends, and acquaintances, what do you think most people would say is the most unique

thing about you? For what qualities would you like to be remembered?

2. Kyle Petty says that excellence is "meeting God's expectations." What do you think are some of God's expectations for your life? What part does excellence play in your legacy?

3. Read Job 8:8–9. How often do you ask for advice from others? As you strive for excellence, what can you gain by following the admonition found in Job 8:8–9? How has paying attention to "the previous generation" taught you a valuable lesson about athletics or life in general?

4. Read Proverbs 13:22. What are some examples of "an inheritance" that someone could leave to his or her children and grandchildren? What kind of inheritance or treasure (whether physical or spiritual) do you hope to leave those who follow in your footsteps?

5. Read Psalm 61:5–8. What does David suggest are some key elements to a godly legacy? What are some of the blessings that accompany that kind of lifestyle? How does having the wrong focus (worrying about what others think of you) hinder your legacy?

Thanks

Fellowship of Christian Athletes would like to give honor and glory to our Lord and Savior Jesus Christ for the opportunities we have been given to impact so many lives and for everyone who has come alongside us in this ministry.

The Four Core values are at the heart of what we do and teach. Many people have helped make this series of books on these values a reality. We extend a huge thanks to Chad Bonham for his many hours of hard work in interviewing, writing, compiling, and editing. These books would not have been possible without him. Thanks also to Chad's wife, Amy, and his three sons, Lance, Cole, and Quinn.

We also want to thank the following people and groups for their vital contributions: Tony Dungy, Kyle Petty, Richard Petty, Davis Hovis, Susan L. Williams, Richard Petty Motorsports, Albert Pujols, Rick Horton, Melody Yount, Jean Driscoll, Roy Helu Jr., Gordon Thiessen, and Lauren Holiday.

Thanks to the entire FCA staff, who faithfully serve coaches and athletes every day. Thanks to our CEO and president, Les Steckel, for believing in this project. Thanks to Jeff Martin, Shea Vailes, Julie Martin, and the entire National Support Center staff. Thanks also to everyone at Revell.

Impacting the World for Christ through Sports

Since 1954, the Fellowship of Christian Athletes has challenged athletes and coaches to impact the world for Jesus Christ. FCA is cultivating Christian principles in local communities nationwide by encouraging, equipping, and empowering others to serve as examples and make a difference. FCA reaches more than two million people annually on the professional, college, high school, junior high, and youth levels. Through FCA's Four Cs of Ministry—Coaches, Campus, Camp, and Community—and the shared passion for athletics and faith, lives are changed for current and future generations.

Fellowship of Christian Athletes
8701 Leeds Road
Kansas City, MO 64129
   www. fca.org
   fca@fca.org
   1-800-289-0909

Fellowship of Christian Athletes
Competitor's Creed

I am a Christian first and last.

I am created in the likeness of God Almighty to bring Him glory.

I am a member of Team Jesus Christ.

I wear the colors of the cross.

I am a Competitor now and forever.

I am made to strive, to strain, to stretch and to succeed in the arena of competition.

I am a Christian Competitor and as such, I face my challenger with the face of Christ.

I do not trust in myself.

I do not boast in my abilities or believe in my own strength.

I rely solely on the power of God.

I compete for the pleasure of my Heavenly Father, the honor of Christ and the reputation of the Holy Spirit.

My attitude on and off the field is above reproach—my conduct beyond criticism.

Whether I am preparing, practicing, or playing, I submit to God's authority and those He has put over me.

I respect my coaches, officials, team-mates, and competitors out of respect for the Lord.

My body is the temple of Jesus Christ.

I protect it from within and without.

Nothing enters my body that does not honor the Living God.

My sweat is an offering to my Master. My soreness is a sacrifice to my Savior.

I give my all—all the time.

I do not give up. I do not give in. I do not give out.

I am the Lord's warrior—a competitor by conviction and a disciple of determination.

I am confident beyond reason because my confidence lies in Christ.

The results of my effort must result in His glory.

Let the competition begin.

Let the glory be God's.

Sign the Creed • Go to www.fca.org

Fellowship of Christian Athletes
Coach's Mandate

Pray as though nothing of eternal value is going to happen in my athletes' lives unless God does it.

Prepare each practice and game as giving "my utmost for His highest."

Seek not to be served by my athletes for personal gain, but seek to serve them as Christ served the church.

Be satisfied not with producing a good record, but with producing good athletes.

Attend carefully to my private and public walk with God, knowing that the athlete will never rise to a standard higher than that being lived by the coach.

Exalt Christ in my coaching, trusting the Lord will then draw athletes to Himself.

Desire to have a growing hunger for God's Word, for personal obedience, for fruit of the spirit and for saltiness in competition.

Depend solely upon God for transformation—one athlete at a time.

Preach Christ's word in a Christ-like demeanor, on and off the field of competition.

Recognize that it is impossible to bring glory to both myself and Christ at the same time.

Allow my coaching to exude the fruit of the Spirit, thus producing Christ-like athletes.

Trust God to produce in my athletes His chosen purposes, regardless of whether the wins are readily visible.

Coach with humble gratitude, as one privileged to be God's coach.

Impacting The World
For Christ Through Sports

Since 1954, the Fellowship of Christian Athletes has challenged athletes and coaches to impact the world for Jesus Christ. FCA is cultivating Christian principles in local communities nationwide by encouraging, equipping, and empowering others to serve as examples and make a difference. FCA reaches more than 2 million people annually on the professional, college, high school, junior high, and youth levels. Through FCA's Four Cs of Ministry—coaches, campus, camps, and community—and the shared passion for athletics and faith, lives are changed for current and future generations.

Fellowship of Christian Athletes
8701 Leeds Road • Kansas City, MO 64129
www.fca.org • fca@fca.org • 1-800-289-0909

DEVOTIONAL READINGS
FOR ATHLETES
AND COACHES

that offer memorable, biblical insights
for handling challenges and performing
with God's purposes in mind.

Revell
a division of Baker Publishing Group
www.RevellBooks.com

 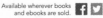